the moon will shine for us too

By Jennae Cecelia

The Moon Will Shine for Us Too

Cover art by Mariah Danielsen of Wander Design Co.
www.wanderdesignco.com

The Moon Will Shine for Us Too

Jennae Cecelia

~

you are messy
& weird.
I love that.

The poetry book you may need, if your darkness seems never ending.

The Moon Will Shine for Us Too
is the sequel to
The Sun Will Rise and So Will We.

I find comfort in a full moon in the middle of autumn, the dead of winter, or after a warm summer day.
But sometimes the darkness comes too early or stays too long, and the only light is in the midnight moon.

Sometimes getting through hard times takes a while. Takes way longer than expected. The darkness may seem overwhelming and the light at the end of the tunnel non-existent, but *The Moon Will Shine for Us Too.*

*I hope the following pages
greet you with comfort.
Know you are welcomed
however messy and weird
you think you are.*

Today you are one step closer
to where you want to go,
while being okay with the fact
that it comes with a lot of unknowns.

How come I can start the day
so motivated and then
the empty shampoo bottle
stares at me in the shower,
but I do not throw it away?
The dish with crusted sauce on it
glares at me,
but I do not wash it away.
My email icon reads 112 new messages,
but I say I will answer another day.
And by 10 AM
my procrastination settles in.
And by 10 PM
I regret all the things I never did.
Tomorrow feels heavy because of
the small tasks I put off.
But I know it
and I keep doing it.
Why can't I stop?

And while everything else
seems to change,
I find comfort in
the sun rising
and setting
the same.

I do not own pajama bottoms
or tops.
And half the week I forget
to take my makeup off.
I drink black coffee
out of mugs that say,
"plant lady" or "dog mom."
I run barefoot down the street
and never properly dress
for the frigid temperatures,
but complain about said temperatures.
And I will catch myself saying,
"I am a mess."
And then I remember,
no, I am me and damn,
I love that.

My mental darkness
likes to make itself known
when the sun falls beneath the trees
and the breeze is ice cold.

I have come too far
to let your opinion of me
scare me into going back
to what felt safe for you.

Your wind tried to push me down
until I was on the ground in need.
But I did not bend to your wind,
and you realized I grew from
a different kind of seed.

I have no desire to be loud
or stand out in a crowd.
I want to blend in.
But here I am not wearing
what they are wearing.
Not smiling like they are.
Not effortlessly beautiful.
And all along
I was never blending in.
I was standing out
by not moving
where everyone else went.

As the darkness comes,
I will remember how
the sun felt on my face.
And I can hold that feeling
long after the moon
has taken its place.

Whether your plans are grand
or unknown,
know that growth
can be made.
It does not matter
if it is fast or slow.

You are allowed to feel
whatever emotions arise
in a season when uncertainty
is at an all-time high.

Stopping will guarantee
never getting there,
but moving with hope
has beautiful possibilities.

I find joy in old linen shirts
from the thrift stores.
Coffee mugs with the perfect
speckled neutral color.
Items that once lived
in someone else's home.
Ready to tell a story all their own.
We all have a story all our own.

How beautiful it is
to wonder why we are here.
Why we get
to breathe in this day
and exhale this night.
I think we are all here
to spread our individual light.

Sometimes I feel like the moon.
Unappreciated.
Unknown.
Unwanted.
Darkness is heavy to hold
and sometimes faking light is easier.
But it only makes it easier
for those viewing you,
while you buckle under the weight
and try to keep moving through.

When you feel like sadness
has made itself a home in you,
remember you cannot truly
welcome in happiness
without sadness knocking
sometimes too.

Without our dark and dreary days
that feel like
they are weighing us down,
how would we ever know
the light and airy days
that came from a time
of so much unknown around?

Maybe today you are wondering
why all of these things
are happening by surprise.
No warning bells.
No signs.
But maybe it has to be a surprise
to get you to *rise*.

Yes, we are on day twelve of just clouds.
No sun in sight.
The silence is loud.
My mind and I are in a fight.
And on these days
when the sun does not shine,
I wait for the moon to be my light.

Just remember when
the lights turn out
and the room is gray.
The light did not give up on you.
It is pausing to soon show you
an even better day.

How will you happily grow
if you do not take the risk
of not tending to
all the worries
you water each day?

Lately it feels like I am stepping
outside with no opportunity to know
what the weather holds.
Do I need an umbrella
to keep me dry,
from my tears
and the sky?
Lack of knowledge.
Lack of control.
Things that do not
go well with an anxious soul.

Maybe this year was supposed to be
the time you finally
blew the dust off your bucket list.
Crossed items off your to-do list.
Just created a list.
Maybe this year you had grand plans
you were eager to meet.
Maybe this year all you did was
wash your face or brush your teeth.
Maybe that was even hard to do.
There is no playbook on how to proceed
when you get hit with
unexpected news,
loss,
or tragedy.
But you being here each day,
well, that is more than enough for me.

Some spaces are not
meant to sparkle and shine.
Some spaces are
meant to show signs
of what goes on
in a creative mind.

It is a heavy load to carry
to be the light
for yourself
and everyone else
who finds the darkness scary.

I do not know why
I make things so hard
when I have come this far.
Why can I not stick to the task?
Why can I not leave things
in the past?
Why must my mind wander
to all the places I no longer
want to visit?
I am tired of getting so far
only for one thing
to push me back in an instance.

Sometimes all you need
to clear your mind
is an open road,
some trees,
and a good breeze.
The simple things
that cost no money.

Something about this
feels like happiness.
It is the sweet smell in the air.
It is the wind
Blowing my hair in every direction.
It is the warmth I soak in
behind closed eyelids.
I could stay like this forever.
Please let me stay like this forever.

Maybe my life looks weird to you.
Maybe my hobbies look weird to you.
Maybe my color choices look weird to you.
Maybe I laugh too weird for you.
Maybe I dream too weird for you.
Maybe you wish you could be this weird too.
Maybe we all need to be as weird as we can.
Maybe that is the answer.
Maybe that is how we feel free.
Maybe life is not supposed to make sense.

Never forget to laugh with joy
at the reflection
you see each day.
Never forget to stare in awe.
You are beautiful art
that first deserves to be
admired by yourself.

You cannot run away from the light forever.
Just when you thought you have
locked yourself in the darkest possible room.
Closed your eyes as tight as you could.
It just took one person
to turn on one light
and it quickly found you.

For all you know.
Maybe that moon is shining
only for you.
Maybe this is all for you.
Maybe you are the main character
and you just have not realized
how crucial you are
to this story yet.

Who cares if they think
you are weird and messy?
Strange and hard to understand.
Only the most beautiful things
have been made out of
the weird and messy.
Only the most beautiful things
have many layers to them.

Maybe no one has told you,
but we all have a dark side
to our moon and nothing about
that makes you less of a person.
Nothing about that makes you horrible.
Nothing about that is wrong.
We all have things we don't
want to be known or shown.
You are not alone in your darkness.

You will find happiness again
even though right now it feels
like you will not greet it anytime soon.
You may feel like you gave it all away.
You may feel like you have not
stopped crying in days.
But that is the great thing
about happiness.
It does not need to make a grand entrance.
Happiness will come to you
in small ways first
and soon you feel like
you gained YOUR happiness back
and not the happiness you put
into other people.

I hope with me,
you feel like you can show up
exactly how you show up
when you are home alone.
Dancing like no one is watching.
Scream singing into a whisk,
pretending it is a microphone.
I hope with me,
you feel like you do not
have to put on a disguise
that you despise.
I hope with me,
you feel as *you*
as you can be.

I am the person who orders
the same coffee drink every day,
but also stares at the menu every day
thinking today may be the day
I make a change.
But then I think about
how changing my drink
may change my whole day.
May change my mood.
Being spontaneous is hard
when you have anxiety.
Even when it is just trying to decide
between switching up simple things
like iced or hot.
Or do I want to add on food or not.

Every time I watch the sun set
I say a silent thank you
for the symbol of a chance to reset.

Maybe this stage of your life looks a lot like
eating take-out food on your living room floor
as you light a candle for some "ambience."
Sitting crisscross in sweat pants
that you have not changed in a few days.
No work life balance.
Just work.
Life.
Fuck, I hope I do not fall.
Balance.
But that is the thing.
This is just a stage in your life.
And maybe you are walking through it
with wobbly legs that resemble
you coming home from the bar.
But one day this will be a stage in your life
you are thankful for.

Some places are not meant
to be left with a reason.
Some places are only meant
to last a season.

This will not be the last hard day.
It is not the first hard day.
But what happened between those days?
Things got better.
There was less rain.
Hard days come.
But they never fully stay.

Maybe you have said you will start today
every day for the last year.
And you are beating yourself up
each day for not following through.
But look at you.
A whole year later still showing up
with the eagerness to grow.
Now think about what that persistence
could manifest into,
if you follow through
and let go.

Sometimes being unsure while you move
is the only way to start getting somewhere.
Imagine if we all waited until
we were perfectly ready to show up.
If we all waited until we were not scared.

Dear Past Me,

I just want you to know
that your sun rose
even though you thought
it never would.
You did not just chase your dreams,
you got them.
You found your beauty in the areas
you saw as flaws.
I cannot wait for you to meet this *you*.

Love,
Present Me

There is hope when the sun hits
the tops of the trees.
When the light peaks through the windows
and coats the room like honey.
Something about it feels
undeserving,
underrated,
and warming.

I found beauty here in the midnight moon.
A chance to recharge.
A chance to quietly bloom.

I remind myself as the sun fades away
that it was never mine to make stay.
You were never mine to make stay.

No one told me what I am supposed to do
when waiting for things to change
seems like once in a blue moon.
I find myself settling into the darkness
and thinking it is what it is.
Will the light come soon?

Today I surrender all of
my need for control.
Take me wherever the wind blows.
I promise I will not question it.
I promise I will not ask why.
I promise I want this.
I am sick of being a prisoner in my mind.

I will point out every full moon
or colorful sunrise.
I will never take for granted again
the beauty of what I thought were
the simple things in my life.

Here is the thing about starting your hike,
the mountains are always waiting for you.
They are always in sight.
The dirt paths will still be there waiting
for you to kick up the dust.
If you need one more day,
that is okay.
The mountains will wait for you.
The mountains never go away.

When will people realize
I have never been shy.
I have so much to say.
My mind is dancing with stories
that want to come out and play.
But how can I talk
when you are much louder
and want to be heard
much more than I do.
So, I sit in silence,
listen,
and silently roll my eyes
when they say,
"don't be shy."

And at the end of the day
all you are left with is you.
Do you love that person?
Do you tell them you do?
What a hard life it will be
if you are enemies with
someone you cannot leave.

There is something about the way
the moon shines in the darkness.
Like it is waiting to hear secrets.
Like it is waiting for you
to know it is okay.
The moon gets you vulnerable.
The moon will have you saying
at 8 AM, "did I really let someone in."
The moon will have you feeling less afraid.

Imagine how good you would feel
if you allowed yourself the same
forgiveness each day
as the earth does the sun
when it parts ways.

I am not trying to be a champagne flute
with something perfectly bubbly enough
for you inside.
I am a mug made by the hands
of someone with a story.
A chip here and there.
Character.
Picked from the shelf and placed
on a creaking wood table with a wobbly leg.
I am not perfect.
But I do not want to be.

Do not worry,
I am not leaving for good.
Breathe.
I am not leaving for good.
I will be back,
even better than before.
I will be back by the time
you walk out the door.
Give me the time I need.
I promise it will be worth
waiting for.

-the sun

I can wish you well
without wishing you back into my life.
I have closed that chapter.
Now the future looks bright.

You called me crazy
and lazy
because I did not agree
with your every word
and I didn't do what
you wanted me to do.
So I closed the door
and said,
"screw you."

Maybe there is not any point to all of this.
Maybe there is no need to do anything grand.
Maybe there is not more to the story.
But I am not waiting
until it is too late to find out,
so I am here every day
trying to move and expand.

How lovely is it that the earth
naturally gives us fresh starts?
From the sun setting.
To the stars rising.
To the rain falling.
A chance to start again and again.

I find myself telling the most stories
from my highest of highs
and my lowest of lows.
Maybe that just shows
that we have to go through it all.
That is how we grow.

Everyone deserves to be told
that they are a star shining
for someone else
that will not let it out of sight.

I gave you the stars,
the moon,
the sun,
and you still said
it was not good enough.
You still said I was not good enough.

You tell me that I am brave,
but I am not.
I have just gotten good at walking
through messy places
while pretending to smile.
I have done this a lot.

I am tired of wanting to be
people that are not me.
I am tired of being told
that who I see on my phone,
is who I am supposed to be.

You are music to me.
I cannot see you,
but I hear you in every word.
Every beat.

Come back to me
when all of the worries you have
come true.
Odds are,
I will never see you.

I cannot tell you to keep going
while I drag behind.
I cannot keep being the motivator.
I cannot keep being the light.
Sometimes I need my own cheerleader.
Sometimes I need to be reminded
not to lose sight.

You can keep saying
you are just one person.
One soul.
So small.
But here you are, taking up space
and impacting lives.
Holding up walls.
Whether you like it or not
you are a person here
impacting other people.
And you not being here
has a ripple effect much bigger than
any small movement you have imagined.

So much has changed since last year.
If it was not for that captured moment
I would not even remember her.

I hope you know that
the things about yourself
that you worry about most
are the things I love
and cannot stop thinking about.

There is nothing better
to be for a friend
than a cheerleader for their success.
Do not be the person playing pretend.
while envying all the places they went.

If your younger self
was sitting across from you today,
would you try to make them proud
or would you push them away?

No one has a story
that is more important to be heard.
We all have stories made for pages.
Made for books.
Made for shelves.
We all have something
someone else needs to hear.
We all are worthy of writing
a book about ourselves.

You do not owe anyone anything.
You are allowed to show up
however you please.
This is not about them.
It is okay if they disagree.

I hope this year brings laughs
that make your stomach hurt
and smiles that leave wrinkles
around your eyes.
I hope this year you take the steps
to find what YOUR happiness is.
I hope this year
you take the world by surprise.

You do not have to change
or have big lofty goals
to be welcomed into this year.
Come as you are right here.

I will no longer allow myself
to mask my pain,
hide my ache,
ignore warning signs
from my brain.
It is time to recognize
when I need a break,
and not feel guilty
or less than.
That has been
my biggest mistake.

As the sun begins to rise,
I feel it lifting my chin up to say,
"things are coming now
that are brighter and better
than you ever imagined yesterday."

There is no such thing
as a happy ending.
Just a happy chapter.
With each page turned,
a new story begins.
Happiness and sadness
are not places you fully land.

Moving forward with hope
will only lead to places
you once thought you could never go.
Moving forward at all
will get you at least somewhere closer
to where you want to know.

Do not ignore your pain.
Sit with it.
Feel it.
Address it.
Pushing it down
only causes it to build up
and erupt one day.

Rumors spread that you changed.
That you are no longer like
who you were yesterday.
If those rumors spread,
do not worry what
they say about you.
You changed into someone
you always wanted to be,
and they no longer fit
into your story like they want to.

Just imagine if life only keeps
getting better from here.
Oh, the stories
you will be able to tell.
Oh, the amount of times
you must have faced your fears.

Even if every year
the seeds I plant do not grow,
I will keep planting them
because one day
just think all that
I will have to show.

Do you want to be the person
that gets excited for other people
or do you want to be the person
that judges from a distance?
Nothing is great about the latter.
It will leave you feeling guilty in an instant.

You made it way too far
to give up now.
To turn around.
Do not go back towards
where you came from,
because I do not think
you will want what you think
may be back there.
Things changed.
You changed.
It no longer fits you.
It is not your place.
It is not the same.

I cannot wait to see
the garden that blooms out of you
when you nurture yourself
and recognize the beauty
that has always been
there to shine through.

I will meet you one year from now
in the park for coffee.
I cannot wait to hear how much
things have changed.
I cannot wait to tell you
all that the year taught me.

I thank the stars for showing up
on nights when I needed
just a speck of hope.
Just a little light to keep me
from giving up this fight.

This season will be golden for you.
I am affirming it for you.
I hope you are ready
for your dreams to come true.
I hope you are ready to soak in
your breakthrough.

If only we looked at ourselves
the same way
that we stare in awe
of the sun setting
as the waves crash
against the bay.

The people who smile the most
are also the people
who may need someone
to smile more at them.
The people who act
the most positive
may have negative thoughts
in their minds.
We all have on a little disguise
when the room is brightly lit
and there is no place to fully hide.

Tell that person you love them.
Say yes to the exciting opportunity
you are nervous about.
Talk to the person
you haven't reached out to in a while,
but keep saying you will soon.
Make that call.
Say that yes.
Love and let go of that grudge.
Savor the now.
Sitting in,
 "what if" land
is the worst feeling.
Tomorrow is only a thought,
not a guarantee.

Get out of the shallow end.
Go deep within yourself.
Go deep within others.
Surface level is safe,
but that is not the right place.

Rain brings growth.
A chance to flush out the old
to make room for the new.
To appreciate the sun-filled days more.
To provide an even better view.

I want to be around more people
that mean it when they say,
"come over any time."
"I miss you."
"let's do this more."
Because that all seems to change
when I come knocking at the door.
Were the 80's movies lies?
Do people not actually spontaneously show up,
for a drive through the fall woods
or to vent their problems
while you pour coffee into their cup?
No questions asked.
Just real connections.
When did we all become so disconnected?

Maybe one day
you will look back and say,
"that was the year that got me here."
Right now, it may be hard to see
as things get canceled
and there is no guarantee.
But one day it could be so obvious
why it needed to happen.
One day it will all make sense
even though right now,
being mad seems like
the only reasonable reaction.

Most days I have no clue
what the hell I am doing
or where I am going.
But I am realizing that is the exciting part.
I have something to work towards every day
even if I do not know right now
what that something is.
I know I will be thankful for these days
I worked so hard even when I was not sure
where it would get me.

The leaves are falling in forgiveness
to make room for new beginnings.

The unexpected paths are okay.
In fact, sometimes they are even better.
So I am walking
barefoot through wildflowers
ready to embrace it all.
Ready for any weather.

What if it was just yourself
left to be inspired by?
Would you find that inspiration
within you?
Could you go without
someone else's advice?
What would that look like?
Would you be alright?

I know you are afraid of
the sun setting and the darkness
settling all too soon.
But just remember,
the moon will shine for us too.

Jennae Cecelia

The Moon Will Shine for Us Too

~

thank you for
giving my words
a home on your shelf
♡ Jennae

To read more work by Jennae Cecelia, check out her other eight books:

The Sun Will Rise and So Will We

Losing Myself Brought Me Here

Dear Me at Fifteen

I Am More Than My Nightmares

Uncaged Wallflower- Extended Edition

I Am More Than a Daydream

Uncaged Wallflower

Bright Minds Empty Souls

About the Author

www.JennaeCecelia.com

@JennaeCecelia on Instagram

@JennaeCecelia on TikTok

Jennae Cecelia is a best-selling author
of inspirational poetry books
and is best known for her books,
The Sun Will Rise and So Will We
and *Uncaged Wallflower*.

She is also an inspirational speaker
who digs into topics like
self-love, self-care, mental health,
and body positivity.

Her mission is to encourage people
to reach their full potential and
live a life filled with positivity and love.

Printed in Great Britain
by Amazon